# ABANDONED
# SOUTHERN
# CALIFORNIA
## THE SLOWING OF TIME

KEN LEE

AMERICA
THROUGH TIME®
ADDING COLOR TO AMERICAN HISTORY

America Through Time is an imprint of Fonthill Media LLC
www.through-time.com
office@through-time.com

Published by Arcadia Publishing by arrangement with Fonthill Media LLC
For all general information, please contact Arcadia Publishing:
Telephone: 843-853-2070
Fax: 843-853-0044
E-mail: sales@arcadiapublishing.com
For customer service and orders:
Toll-Free 1-888-313-2665

www.arcadiapublishing.com

First published 2019

Copyright © Ken Lee 2019

ISBN 978-1-63499-192-6

Typeset in Mrs Eaves XL Serif Narrow
Printed and bound in England

# CONTENTS

# ACKNOWLEDGMENTS

A tip of the hat to the artists and designers of all those amazing airplanes, automobiles, buildings, locomotives, machinery, and more. Your design is the inspiration for much of the photography in this book. And props to the people who carved out an existence in the Southern California desert, digging, building, sweating, and enduring the elements.

Thank you to Joe Davis at Eagle Field, Bill Johnson at Santa's Village, and Mark Wheeler from Desert Institute in Joshua Tree National Park for allowing me to photograph these amazing places. Thank you to fellow night photographers Tim Little, Mike Cooper, Dave Dasinger, George Loo, Ron Pinkerton, Steve McIntyre, and more for your inspiration, knowledge, friendship, and encouragement. Also, thank you to the Facebook communities, including Long Exposure Photography and Long Exposure Creativity, for creating a forum to meet other night photographers and to learn, share, and grow together.

Enormous gratitude to the night photographer I met in 2000. I do not know who you are, but I stopped by your booth on the Venice Boardwalk in Los Angeles to see your display of night photography prints of Joshua Tree. Although I wouldn't try it with any seriousness until twelve years later, you planted the seed of night photography by describing your forty-five-minute long-exposure night photos, how you created the shadows on the Joshua Tree rocks, and by insisting, "You know, there's more light at night than you think there is." I had no idea what a huge influence you would have on me, and I only wish that I could see you again so I could thank you.

Maximum respect to Troy Paiva and Lance Keimig. When I was discovering examples of night photography online, your pioneering images were the ones that inspired me the most, first seen through the Lost America and Nocturnes websites. Your books have been inspirational and educational. And more importantly, thank you for your encouragement and friendship.

Thank you to Jay Slater and Alan Sutton and everyone at Fonthill Media for giving me this opportunity. And thanks to Lisa Kelly, my friends and family for encouraging me to explore, believe, and be me.

# CREATING THE IMAGES

The images in this book were created at night with long-exposure photography techniques. I use a Nikon DSLR mounted on a sturdy tripod. When creating an image, I leave the shutter open for up to several minutes, often long enough to show the stars streaking across the night sky and allowing whatever light is available to "soak in" a bit.

While the shutter is open, I use a handheld ProtoMachines LED2 flashlight, capable of creating different colors, to illuminate the scene, choosing what to highlight and what to leave in shadow. Some of my early photographs were lit in a similar manner using a Streamlight LED flashlight and theatrical lighting gels. All the lighting is done in-camera at the time of exposure, and is not the product of post-processing enhancement techniques.

Many of these night images are colorful. Some who are not familiar with night photography might regard this as odd since this isn't the way night typically appears to our eyes. As night grows darker, our eyes become increasingly monochromatic. Our retinas widen to let in more light. But while our cones function well in brighter light and see color, our rods are monochromatic. However, our camera does not have the same limitations as our eyes, registering colors in low light far more vividly.

Not much equipment is needed to create these images. Indeed, all of it can fit in a small backpack, leaving me free to explore on foot easily. Typically, I have a camera, tripod, flashlight, batteries, snacks, water, and not much else. This allows me to move easily, create, and photograph these historic treasures before the elements or bulldozers erase them from existence.

# INTRODUCTION

I n past decades, dreams have flourished in the deserts of Southern California, fueled by gold, war, optimism, and wealth, only to later be abandoned. Homes, mines, utopian societies, railroads, airports, airplanes, cars, gas stations, and more were eventually discarded. Already a place of mystery, the desert seems even more so at night as shadows wander, winds whisper, and stars slowly swim across the sky.

Southern California has generally been a place of optimism. It is largely the financial engine that drives the United States. The region launched car culture and the film industry and is one of the largest media centers in the world. The military and aeronautics industry made their home here. It is a place where immigrants arrive, bringing with them their hopes and dreams and endurance.

However, many people who held these dreams eventually departed, leaving their belongings unguarded and forgotten. Airfields, once necessary for World War II, became relics of the past, surrounded by farmland. Resorts for the rich and famous on the shores of the Salton Sea were abandoned when the sea began to decay. Utopian societies dried up when their water supplies did. Miners left their homes and saloons when the earth stopped giving up its riches. Gas stations and restaurants shuttered their windows when new highways left them ignored. Airplanes past their prime were dismantled or forgotten. All these were left to the desert winds, the dust, the sun, and the passing of time.

Exploring these decaying dreams during the day can be strange. But at night, it is otherworldly. Moonlight, starlight and shadows intermingle with silence, dust and rust. You enter a dark, creaky room, and a sudden rustling of bats brushes past you. Corrugated metal screeches, breaking the desert silence. The echo of coyotes reverberates in the rocky canyons. Mysterious flashlights wobble in the distance.

Photographing in abandoned areas fills you with adventure, wonder, curiosity, or alarm. Your senses are heightened. You are, after all, exploring in the dark. It becomes even more crucial to be careful, to wear boots with steel shank soles, to carefully test the floor, to hope you know where to go, and to hope you know when to leave.

I am always asked if I am afraid of encountering animals or ghosts. No, not so much. I am more concerned with encountering people. Exploring at night increases the likelihood of meeting explorers, weirdos, partiers, squatters, drunkards, security guards, or police. Friendliness, respect and courtesy go a long way. So does showing examples of my night photos to set some at ease. And yes, so does knowing when to leave.

Photographing at night also offers a curious compression of time through the process of creating long exposures. Long exposures allow me to illuminate these abandoned places for several minutes, allowing me to act almost as a film director. I am able to convey a sense of mystery by choosing what to highlight with a handheld flashlight and choosing what to leave in shadow during long exposure images that can be minutes or even hours in length. I find it fascinating to be able to represent this cumulative illumination and passage of time in a single image.

But another sort of compression of time seems to occur, a result of the creative, deliberate process of long exposure photography as much as the desert night, where hours pass like minutes, the very act often meditative. When I create photos for hours in the dark of night, I slow down and connect with the surroundings – a luxury in such a stressful world. Whether experimenting with just one more lighting setup or realizing that I can actually perceive the directions in which the stars drift across the sky, the feeling is often transportive. And although I love the feeling of adventure and wonder, it is so often the creative and meditative qualities that beckon me to return.

# 1

# EAGLE FIELD

With the escalation of World War II, the United States War Department began contracting with civilian flight schools to train pilots for the army. One of these facilities was Eagle Field. Construction in the broad flat desert in the San Joaquin Valley began in 1942. Boasting steam heat, air conditioning, a soda machine, landscaping, and a recreation hall, Eagle Field was a rather comfortable place for training. Five thousand pilots graduated from Eagle Field after thirty months of training, with only three lives lost due to accidents, an excellent record. Many civilians were employed at the airfield.

However, Eagle Field's fortunes soon changed. As the Allied war effort grew successful and after many pilots had been trained, contracts were canceled at the airfield. The last cadets left at the end of 1944. After this, the town of Dos Palos attempted to convert Eagle Field into a municipal airport but failed, with the property reverting to the federal government in the 1970s. In 1980, it was put up for auction. Much of it was purchased by Joe Davis, who has worked since then to restore the airfield out of respect for the men and women who helped win the war.

Mr. Davis was kind enough to let several of my friends and me photograph here at night, helping us with logistics and advice, and generally trusting us with the run of the place, and for that we are grateful. The area has an amazing array of vintage airplanes and much more, including an old fuel truck labeled "Aeropuerto de Nazca", used in an Indiana Jones movie when the protagonist was in Peru.

A fisheye view of a fuel truck used in a 2008 *Indiana Jones* movie, part of which was filmed at Eagle Field.

Another fisheye view of the fuel truck, this time using a colored flashlight to illuminate the interior of the truck.

A Fokker D.VI German single-seat fighter aircraft from WWI, located inside the hangar.

Another view of the Fokker D.VI German single-seat fighter aircraft from WWI. Much of the airplane frame was constructed of wood with fabric covering, seeming surprisingly lightweight.

The Spirit of the San Joaquin. This is another fisheye view of the Lockheed Harpoon at Eagle Field.

Taylorcraft airplane. Because this is missing its wings, I found myself thinking about it as a helicopter.

The interior of the Taylorcraft Airplane.

Peering into the window of an airplane, lit with blue light from my handheld flashlight during the exposure, careful to not disturb the nesting birds inside.

The interior of a helicopter.

The remains of a cockpit.

The interior of a large aircraft.

A fighter plane and an MG inside the hangar.

A dusty Jaguar XK convertible located inside the cavernous hangar.

This car apparently had no takers for $800. This is one of many old cars parked outside the hangar at Eagle Field.

An old 1950s
Bennett gas pump
rusting away.

Oldsmobile Super 88.

Part of the 2008 *Indiana Jones* movie was filmed at this hangar.

An old Riley. My arm was covered with spider webs after sticking my arm in the window to illuminate the interior. This is one of the many joys of photographing abandoned things at night.

Iron Butterfly, a Vietnam-era helicopter in the hangar.

An airplane fuel tanker seemingly peering at the nearby fields.

# 2

# JOSHUA TREE NATIONAL PARK

For many visitors to Southern California's famed Joshua Tree National Park, driving along Park Boulevard and stopping along the way is satisfying. Of course, there is much more to the Park than this. Within the boundaries, there are many abandoned areas, some well-known, some obscure, and some secret.

Ryan Ranch, an adobe structure built in 1896 by the family of J.D. Ryan, is a well-known feature of Joshua Tree National Park. Unfortunately, it was destroyed by fire in August 1978. The family also developed the nearby Lost Horse Mine.

Ohlson Ranch is known for its pink walls. However, not much else is known about the ranch. When I photographed this at night, we had just arrived from Jumbo Rocks, which was noticeably warmer. Ohlson Ranch, on the other hand, was around freezing, and we noticed that there were discernible pockets of particularly cold air around the ranch.

Deep within the Park boundaries are a dozen cars that are half-buried in sand, far away from any road or trail. I have never been able to find much history on this, as people are rather tight-lipped about this area, but it appears to be associated with a mine, and it's possible that the cars may have been stranded by a flood or belonged to an extremely remote car repair place that was simply abandoned.

Also hidden from most visitors are Samuelson's Rocks, eight rocks on a hill engraved with strange messages. Photographing this at night required a mile-long walk along the desert with no trails. I was grateful for my handy GPS, but not so grateful for the cactus that poked through my boot on the return trip. John Samuelson was a miner and rancher for the Keys Ranch. In the 1920s, he built a cabin and began carving messages into the rocks. He eventually moved with his wife to Los Angeles, where he killed two people in Compton. He was declared insane, but later escaped from the hospital.

Carey's Castle, or Cary's Castle, requires a four-mile hike and a bit of boulder scrambling while going up sandy washes. I have only visited this during the day, but these were too good not to share with you despite my wanting to have only night photos.

This fascinating home, originally a cave used by Native Americans for shelter, was built in the 1930s by Arthur Loyd Cary, who added walls and windows. Although we often think of desert prospectors as grizzled, Cary was about twenty-four years old when he built this after staking several mining claims nearby. For the longest time, this was one of the huge secrets of Joshua Tree National Park, the stuff of legend, with many looking for it, but few finding it due to its remote location. However, it became reasonably well-known, with numerous sites posting GPS coordinates. Unfortunately, due to vandalism, it is closed to the public as of this writing.

**OPPOSITE PAGE**

▲ Ryan Ranch underneath the Milky Way, Joshua Tree National Park. This was the main house, which unfortunately caught fire in August 1978, destroying most of the structure. Arson was suspected, but never determined.

▼ The adobe walls of Ryan Ranch. This ranch is one of the most accessible historical ruins in the park, a short walk from the main road. Unfortunately, this has resulted in vandalism, which you can see here.

**PREVIOUS PAGE**

▲ Ohlson Ranch, known for its pink walls.

▼ Ohlson Ranch.

Ohlson Ranch. I would love to wake up to a view of a gorgeous Joshua Tree and stunning rock formations.

One of several vehicles half-buried in sand, far from any road or trail. This is arguably one of the more unknown and mysterious places inside the park.

## OPPOSITE PAGE

▲ One of several cars half-buried in sand in a rather dramatic manner.

▼ An upside-down Cadillac half-buried in sand.

Samuelson's Rocks. On this evening, I walked about a mile in the dark, before the moon had risen, relying upon my GPS since I could not see the rocks. To my surprise, I encountered two young men setting up camp in front of this rock. They had seen my flashlight in the distance and were alarmed that I appeared to be headed their way. I told them I had been hoping to photograph Samuelson's Rocks, but understood that they had already set up camp. After determining that I wasn't a threat, they agreed to temporarily move their belongings so I could photograph the rock. I worked quickly, thanking them while doing so.

Samuelson's Rocks. Back in 1927, John Samuelson unfortunately did not have access to spellcheck.

Samuelson's Rocks, wondering about where his money went.

Cary's Castle, one of the three daytime photos in this book. Visiting this area requires a four-mile hike and some light boulder scrambling, although currently, Cary's Castle has been closed due to vandalism.

The interior of Cary's Castle. There are petroglyphs on the ceiling from when Native Americans used this small cave for shelter.

A close-up of Cary's Castle's door, which may no longer exist. Some locals say that it was used for firewood.

# 3

# MINERS OF THE MOJAVE

The Gold Rush in California has been romanticized, the subject of countless books and movies. Many other minerals are mined in California as well, including boron, sodium, and gypsum. Consequently, there have been countless mines in Southern California.

Between 1910 and 1969 in what is now Joshua Tree National Park, Bill Keys built Keys Ranch for homesteading, cattle ranching, farming, and of course, mining. He even started the first grade school in Joshua Tree. Keys was ambushed in his car by Worth Bagley. He returned fire, killing Bagley. He was sent to jail, but was released from prison five years later. This ranch is carefully guarded by rangers today, and is only available by tour.

In Dublin Gulch in Shoshone, miners carved residences in the sides of cliffs since building materials were in short supply. Some believe that they were built in the 1920s, although a few feel they were dug out in the late 1870s when silver was discovered in a nearby mine. Some of the dugouts have chimneys and doors, and at least one has a garage. Nobody has lived in Dublin Gulch since 1970.

Tecopa was named for Chief Tecopa, the leader of the Southern Paiute group of Native Americans. Mining began here in the 1860s, and by 1880, Tecopa had a ten stamp mill and three furnaces. Many workers hauled ore, silver, and lead out of the earth until the 1950s by Tecopa Consolidated Mining Company. Today, Tecopa might be best known for its hot springs.

Prospectors named the Alabama Hills in Owens Valley after a Confederate ship. The Hills have unusual shapes, many with arches, and have been a popular destination for movie makers since the 1920s. A number of dugouts in the area housed explosives.

Trona Pinnacles is an otherworldly location noted for its odd-shaped tufas left over from the remains of an ancient lake bed. Many science fiction movies have been filmed here. And here, miners came for borax.

Garlock is a mining ghost town that was also known as El Paso City or Cow Wells. When a nugget of gold was found in 1893, the inevitable rush began, and Eugene

Garlock brought in an eight stamp mill. At its height, Garlock had a couple of bars and hotels, a school, a laundry, and a doctor's office.

High above the parched sands of Death Valley National Park are the Wildrose Charcoal Kilns, built in 1877. In mountains towering more than 8000 feet above the desert floor, these twenty-five foot tall kilns were used only for a couple of years, which might account for their excellent condition. Almost 150 years later, one can still smell the burnt charcoal. Constructed by the Modock Consolidated Mine Company, the kilns provided fuel for smelters in their lead and silver mines in nearby Panamint Valley, transported by wagon and donkey pack-trains. We photographed these kilns on a cold December evening.

Mines and mining towns such as these and many more dot Southern California. Some can be found readily, others from looking at old maps, but many are lost to history and Mojave dust.

Some of the historic cars at Keys Ranch at night, located near mining equipment in what is now Joshua Tree National Park.

Bill Keys of Keys Ranch was ambushed in this car by Worth Bagley. Keys returned fire, killing Bagley. One can see a pockmark from one of Bagley's bullets on the other side of the car.

The Keys Ranch store at night.

An old historic 29 Palms Produce bottle on the backside of the interior store.

The Keys Ranch home during a cloudy evening.

Miners' residences carved into the sides of cliffs at Dublin Gulch in Shoshone, illuminated by a full moon and the stars drifting across the night sky over time. These residences have been abandoned since 1970, according to locals.

A couple of miners' residences carved into the sides of cliffs at Dublin Gulch. The faint downward streak seen at the upper left of the North Star is a meteor lighting up the night sky.

Miners' residences, Dublin Gulch.

The U-We Wash, an abandoned laundromat located in the old mining town of Tecopa, founded in 1878. I walked inside to illuminate the interior with an eerie blue light. There are still many laundry machines inside in various states of disrepair.

An abandoned Ford truck at night, lit with some colored lights from various angles while the camera shutter was open, giving the illusion of working headlights, among other things. This is located in front of the abandoned laundromat in Tecopa.

The cab of an abandoned Ford truck, Tecopa.

▲ A dugout in the Alabama Hills in Owens Valley used to house explosives for mining.

▼ A dugout in the Alabama Hills. I especially love the unusual rock formations of the hill. The dugout appears like a gate from hell due to red light from my handheld flashlight illuminating the interior of the dugout.

The otherworldly tufas of Trona Pinnacles near Ridgecrest. While I cannot find any specific information on this dugout online, someone who saw my photo commented that his father built this for housing explosives. When I photographed this at night, I was startled by some bats shooting past me as I entered the dugout. Many times while photographing natural or abandoned places, I have been startled by birds, bats, rats, or other animals, one of the exciting aspects of night photography.

The remains of an abandoned mine located in Antelope Valley. I am not certain of the name of this mine, as we came across it while exploring.

There's not much to watch on TV tonight in this old miner's house located in Antelope Valley.

The old mining ghost town of Garlock. The "no trespassing" sign might not be necessary for many when coupled with a "rattlesnake area" sign.

The rusty water tower in Garlock ghost town.

## PREVIOUS PAGE

▲ The Wildrose Charcoal Kilns in Death Valley National Park. I could still smell the burnt charcoal from almost 150 years ago.

▼ The Wildrose Charcoal Kilns. We photographed these during a very cold December evening at 8,000 feet in elevation. On another visit, I met someone playing an African stringed instrument in one of the kilns, taking advantage of its beautiful, unique acoustic properties.

The Wildrose Charcoal Kilns.

# 4

# MOVIE SETS OF THE MOJAVE

**M**ost people know that Southern California is one of the foremost movie capitals of the world. Studio sets have been built all around the region. With this many sets, it's inevitable that some are eventually abandoned, whether for financial reasons, poor choices, or simply because the studio didn't want to break it down and haul it away. I was sworn to secrecy by the person who took me here, but regardless, I can't seem to find much information about the studio or what was filmed or made here. Most of what I saw at night looked Roman or Greek, and the location was littered with columns, busts, statues, reliefs, and stands as well as plaster molds. I will leave you to enjoy these night photos of this movie studio, wondering about what sort of films were made here, when they were made, and why this place was abandoned.

**OPPOSITE PAGE**

▲ Columns at a mysterious abandoned movie set located deep in the Mojave Desert. Many sources state that this was an abandoned movie set, although some say it was actually home to a sculptor.

▼ Columns at a mysterious movie set, underneath the glow of a full moon. Several years later, I returned to this area to find that many of the columns had fallen over and broken.

## PREVIOUS PAGE

▲ Crumbling statues greet the night at a mysterious abandoned movie set.

▼ A gargoyle and fallen column underneath some thick trees at a mysterious movie set.

Another view of the columns from an abandoned movie set.

# 5

# CAR CULTURE

Southern California embraced car culture with a hug and a kiss. Close your eyes and you can visualize cars of yesteryear with their enormous fins cruising across long ribbons of highway. Some of these automobiles are now prized possessions of car collectors, while others rust underneath the open sky throughout the Southland. Most of these photos are from auto salvage yards.

The interior of a large 1950s ice cream truck at an auto salvage yard in the Mojave Desert.

## OPPOSITE PAGE

▲ A fisheye view of an old Cadillac camper underneath the night sky of the Mojave Desert.

▼ The front view of an old Cadillac camper. You can see some blurring of the hood, which was swaying in the wind during this twenty-minute long exposure.

▲ An old DeSoto, looking as if one of its fins are waving at us.

▼ This truck bed was sawed in half for some inexplicable reason. Its remaining taillight looks ominously at us through the camera's fisheye lens.

A Mercury underneath some beautiful night clouds.

A Buick as seen through a fisheye lens. I used colored lights from various angles while the camera shutter was open.

This is the Knight Rider 2010 "Hannah" car from a made-for-TV movie taking place in a Mad Max-style future, loosely based on the TV series, but in reality, having little in common with it. The car is an uglified 1991 Thunderbird.

A Chrysler Windsor, a car made from 1939 through the 1960s.

The front of a DeSoto, lit from various angles while the camera shutter was open.

## PREVIOUS PAGE

▲ A rather textured front hood of a Plymouth.

▼ Canted quad headlights of a 1962 Chrysler Newport peer out into the night.

A rather bent view of an old Edsel, courtesy of my fisheye lens.

An abandoned security van.

The back of an old electrical services work truck.

Taillights of an old Edsel.

Several trucks saluting the incoming clouds.

▲ Spectacular night clouds over an auto salvage yard in the Mojave Desert.

▼ A one-eyed Dodge with some amazing cloud formations sweeping across the night desert sky.

Rusting underneath the night sky, its headlights aiming in directions not originally intended by the manufacturer.

## PREVIOUS PAGE

▲ The clouds almost appear to be rising out of the back trunk.

▼ A rusty dislodged hood illuminated by a combination of moonlight, handheld light, and a touch of light added to the headlight.

A 1962 Chrysler Newport at night.

A sort of piggyback ride.

## OPPOSITE PAGE

▲ The 18-foot tall fiberglass Uniroyal Girl greets all passersby. The sculptor apparently modeled her after Jackie Kennedy.

▼ A ghostly self-portrait in an old GM bus, the last photo at the end of a long, creative evening of night photography.

# 6

# WARBIRDS

If magnificent aircraft such as these can be found languishing in the desert, it feels like just about anything can be abandoned. Lost somewhere in the Mojave Desert, I gasped when friends first took me to see these enormous planes. Outside in the cool desert air, I was sometimes startled by loud creaks punctuating the night, the restless desert wind moving the metal in the fuselage or the wings. Otherwise, it was a creative night photographing these historic warbirds.

The broken tail end of a magnificent aircraft underneath the desert night sky.

The tail end of a historic warbird abandoned in the California desert.

One of numerous historic aircraft.

A separated tail of an airplane. As with many things left unattended in the desert, people unfortunately find their way to them with spray cans.

## Opposite page

▲ A separated tail of an airplane during this long-exposure photo showing the movement of the stars.

▼ An abandoned and heavily damaged Air Force plane.

## PREVIOUS PAGE

◄ This image looks like an Air Force plane somehow crashed on another planet.

A separated tail of an airplane underneath the starry desert sky.

## OPPOSITE PAGE

▲ A separated tail of an airplane with the tip pointing at the North Star, showing the apparent movement of stars over many minutes of time.

▼ The moon appearing over one of the wings of this magnificent aircraft shortly after moonrise.

A moon with a gorgeous halo, backlighting a heavily damaged Air Force plane.

## OPPOSITE PAGE

▲ The tail of an abandoned plane as seen through a fisheye lens.

▼ This photo reminds many of a carcass after a whale hunt.

The remains of an airplane seen from the back in this fisheye-view photo.

Another view of an Air Force plane.

Looking directly into the innards of a severed tail of an abandoned airplane.

Looking northward, seeing the apparent movement of the stars over a long period of time in a single image.

# PREVIOUS PAGE

▲ The Friendly Skies. This Air Force plane almost seems like it is smiling.

▼ I added a warm glow to this abandoned airplane with a handheld flashlight while the camera shutter was open.

The Milky Way seen over an Air Force plane.

The Milky Way seen over an Air Force plane, looking as if it has crash-landed on a distant planet.

## OPPOSITE PAGE

A sort of "Batman View" of an abandoned airplane and the glorious Milky Way arching overhead. The view of the Milky Way and these magnificent airplanes of yesteryear would take anyone's breath away.

# 7

# SALTON SEA

S ometimes, human-made accidents profoundly change the land. However, few of them create enormous lakes. The Salton Sea in the Sonoran Desert near the Mexican border is one such accident.

In 1905, engineers from the California Development Company attempted to divert water from the Colorado River via a canal. This water, however, had ideas of its own, and overflowed its banks and flooded a valley that lay below sea level. This eventually became the largest lake by area in California. Soon, fish were introduced to the lake. Tourists and movie stars began flocking here. Motels, resorts, and yacht clubs sprung up. By the 1950s, the area was a greater tourist draw than Yosemite National Park.

However, with no new water and no outlet, the Salton Sea became salty. Worse than that, pesticides and fertilizers from the surrounding agricultural community flowed into the lake, contaminating it. The fish began dying, and so did the birds. As the saline levels and algae increased, the Salton Sea also began to smell, and with that, the tourists dwindled, leaving their motels, swimming pools, yacht clubs, homes, and mineral springs to melt back into the earth.

The Salton Sea has many interesting features near its shores. Salvation Mountain, near the squatters community of Slab City, is one such site. Leonard Knight spent three decades joyously painting religious messages on a tall mountain built with adobe mixed with straw. Knight believed that he had put more than 100,000 gallons of paint on his mountain to combat erosion of wind and rain. Knight passed away in 2014, leaving the future of Salvation Mountain in doubt. The residents of Slab City, including various caretakers, have sometimes fixed up and watched over Salvation Mountain, but since Knight's death, there has been mounting concern about damage from the elements and vandalism.

An abandoned mineral spa, Salton Sea. I illuminated the interior of this main building with a blue light from my handheld flashlight during the exposure.

We felt like we were photographing a bombed-out building from a war-torn city, not a mineral spa near the Mexican border.

The forlorn grounds of an abandoned mineral spa by the Salton Sea.

## OPPOSITE PAGE

▲ One of several structures at an abandoned mineral spa, illuminated with an eerie blue light from my handheld flashlight. There are numerous mineral baths behind this structure.

▼ Inside one of the mineral spas. This had many mud wasps inside and smelled awful, so I was happy to leave. This photo was done in almost complete darkness.

This evoked the remains of a war-torn area, not a mineral spa in decay. The fragile-looking beams on the right had collapsed when I returned to this site a couple of years later.

Bombay Beach on the shores of the Salton Sea. This is one of the remaining structures, many of which seem like they are melting into the earth.

Salvation Mountain, near the Salton Sea, lovingly built by Leonard Knight using adobe mixed with straw and a ridiculous amount of paint.

Salvation Mountain. On another visit, a couple from nearby Slab City, a squatters' community, was exchanging vows and invited us to join the ceremony. Noticing that I had a DSLR, they asked me if I could photograph their wedding, which I was only too happy to do.

One of the trucks continually parked by Salvation Mountain, festooned with messages from Leonard Knight.

**OPPOSITE PAGE**

▲ One of several vehicles decorating Salvation Mountain.

▼ Another view of one of the trucks that always seems to be parked on the premises.

# 8

# DECAYING DREAMS

They came to the desert, dreaming of new beginnings.

Job Halloran dreamed of building a utopian society in the Antelope Valley. He had almost won a bid for mayor of Los Angeles, but soon became disillusioned with politics. Not trusting the political system to enact social change, Harriman founded the Llano Del Rio community in the desert north of Los Angeles in the early 1900s. The cooperative thrived, its population exceeding 1000, until their water supply was diverted by an earthquake fault. They opened one of the country's first Montessori schools, created a fertile intellectual and cultural community, and established innovative low-cost housing, Social Security, minimum-wage pay, and universal health care services that predated the rest of the country by decades. Although Llano del Rio is today considered Western American history's most important non-religious utopian community, there is unfortunately no protection for the site despite being a California Historic Landmark.

Lonnie Coffman dreamed of building a miniature golf course. With the help of Gregory Wicker, the two built dinosaurs of concrete in Apple Valley. This was never finished.

Miners dreamed of making money by shipping ore across the Owens Lake in steamships. Their dreams quite literally dried up along with Owens Lake when the thirsty metropolis of Los Angeles siphoned the water away.

President Franklin Delano Roosevelt dreamed of making citizens feel safe from Americans of Japanese descent by ordering their relocation to concentration camps during World War II. Manzanar in the Owens Valley was one such camp. This guard tower serves as a reminder of our dark past.

Businesspeople dreamed of building restaurants and gas stations in Halloran Springs for motorists driving Interstate 15 between Southern California and Las Vegas.

Glen Holland dreamed of building Santa's Village, a tourist wonderland in the mountains towering above the deserts. A local Crestline resident, he employed local artisans to create the village in 1955. This park opened six weeks before Disneyland, and although high in the mountains, was one of Southern California's largest tourist attractions, boasting a bobsled, monorail, Ferris wheel, petting zoo, live reindeer, and more. When tourism dwindled, the park closed in 1998, barely surviving a fire several years after that.

These remnants of dreams are left for us to imagine what was and what could have been.

The silo at Llano Del Rio, part of the remains of an abandoned utopian society in the Mojave Desert.

PREVIOUS PAGE

▲ Dinosaurs at an abandoned miniature golf course in Apple Valley.

▼ An abandoned RV near what was once the banks of Owens Lake, where mighty steamships once carried ore from Cerro Gordo. The water from the lake and much of Owens Valley was diverted via the Los Angeles aqueduct, leaving it a dry, dusty catastrophe.

An old guard tower at Manzanar in Owens Valley, a former concentration camp for Americans of Japanese ancestry, serving as an ominous reminder of our country's past.

An abandoned restaurant at a former rest stop in Halloran Springs, built to serve motorists driving between Southern California and Las Vegas.

Old rest stop signs, Halloran Springs.

An abandoned shack, possibly a storage shack, Halloran Springs. The streaks of light behind the shack are from headlights on Interstate 15.

An abandoned gas station along Interstate 15 near Yermo.

An abandoned gas station along Interstate 15 near Yermo.

Alta Vista sign from a business long forgotten, Antelope Valley.

Santa's Village on a rather foggy evening. This mountain park was once one of Southern California's largest tourist attractions.

Santa's Village. Built in the 1950s, the village closed in 1998, remaining abandoned for many years.

# ABOUT THE AUTHOR

Night photographer Ken Lee has been exploring the Southwest United States as well as parts of the East Coast for over six years, brandishing a camera, tripod, and colored flashlight. His images have appeared in *National Geographic Books*, *Omni Magazine*, *Los Angeles Times*, *Westways Magazine*, and many other publications. He lives in the Los Angeles area. Learn more about Ken's photography at instagram.com/kenleephotography or facebook.com/kenleephotography.